CONFRONTING
THE PAST

POCKET EDITION

Published from
Mardukite Borsippa HQ, San Luis Valley, Colorado
Mardukite Academy & Systemology Society
for spiritual or educational purposes only

CONFRONTING THE PAST

Systemology
Professional Course
Booklet #9

Developed by Joshua Free
for the Systemology Society

© 2023, JOSHUA FREE

ISBN : 978-1-961509-34-4

Pocket Paperback Edition — *December 2023*

mardukite.com

Chart Your Flight For Ascension...
Then Let Your Spirit Fly!

Unlock your ultimate spiritual potential by removing barriers to your true native state.

Learn how to easily attain Self-actualization and help to actualize others along the way.

A greater appreciation and understanding of *Spiritual Life* and *Existence* awaits you. Expand your reach to achieve your dreams.

Each 'Professional Course' lesson-booklet offers simple exercises and techniques that directly apply the philosophy of Systemology, assisting to increase your true knowingness, improve your capabilities in this life, and even decide what you will do in your next.

At the Mardukite Academy of Systemology, the 'Professional Course' lessons in this series are presented to Seeker's that have already completed the 'Basic Course', previously released as six lesson-booklets, or the six-in-one single volume edition "Fundamentals of Systemology."

This all new presentation of the Systemology 'Pathway-to-Ascension' takes Seekers and continuing students from "Zero" to "Infinity" at lightning-fast speeds!

Discover Who You Really Are...

Because You Were Never Human

TABLET OF CONTENTS

COURSE INTRODUCTION

LESSON NINE:
CONFRONTING THE PAST

APPENDIX

PROFESSIONAL COURSE INTRODUCTION

WELCOME, SEEKER!
LET'S CHART YOUR JOURNEY
ON THE PATHWAY

Systemology is a "holistic" approach to understanding the human experience. It is not actually a singular "subject" in itself, but rather, a new way in which to view the many subjects of *Life* and all *Existence.*

This is a professional course in *Systemology*—specifically, how to *apply* the spiritual philosophy of *Mardukite Systemology* as a personal *"Pathway" to Ascension.* Our *Systemology* is a new approach to *"Self-Actualization."* It is completely relevant for the modern age and the future; and quite different from any previous similar attempts, or other traditions, you might find. What's more: it is applicable to anyone with any background.

This "*Professional Course*" series of lessons (booklets) immediately follows the material given in the "*Basic Course*" series—available as six separate pocket-sized booklets, or in a single hardcover volume titled: "*Fundamentals of Systemology: A New Thought For The 21st Century.*"

This is a *new* presentation of *Systemology*, emphasizing the application of our philosophy for those *Seekers* that are "*Flying-Solo*"—or else working through their studies and exercises as solitary practitioners. This is a new innovation for *Systemology*. Aside from the book "*Crystal Clear*," all of our former advanced courses have placed a focus on "*Traditional Piloting*"—where experienced practitioners assist *Seekers* in "*processing.*"

To receive the greatest benefit from this study: it is expected that a *Seeker* will already be familiar with the fundamental concepts and terminology (previously relayed in the *Basic Course*) before using lessons from the *Professional Course*. This will allow us to cover the extensive territory of the *Pathway* much more quickly. However, for reference, a basic *"glossary"* of vocabulary used in this lesson is provided in the *"appendix."*

A NEW VIEW OF THE HUMAN SPIRIT

Systemology is not a religion and does not require any type of *faith*. It is, however, built upon a "spiritual" premise—and as such is an "applied spiritual philosophy." It is based on ancient teachings that we are *Spiritual Beings* essentially "wearing" bodies like clothes—or using them as "vehicles." Yet our true native nature is not *physical,* but beyond this existence; and we can certainly operate a "body" from *outside* of it.

We are **all** *Spiritual Beings*—each of us a *unit* of *Spiritual Awareness*—that have experienced a very long *Spiritual Timeline* of existence. Although we might be particularly attached to the familiar "physical shells" associated with *this* lifetime, our true *"Spiritual Lifetime"* is seemingly *eternal*. We have been many things before *Human*, and we go onward as a *Spiritual Being* after our *"genetic vehicle"* of *this* incarnation perishes.

While a "spiritual" view of the *Human Condition* may not seem unique to our philosophy, just how often is the concept treated *systematically*? For that matter: just how many people, supposedly raised to this or that religion, or professing to believe one thing or another, actually live their lives as though they are *Spirits?*

As *Spiritual Beings* of immortal existence and infinite potential, we are not simply the *"creations"* of an even greater *Being*-

ness; we are, in fact, an integral part of that *"creative force"* which permeates all existence.

Our basic nature is to be a *"creative being"*—our highest goals are *"to create."* And as such a being—which we refer to as an *Alpha-Spirit* in *Systemology*—we have run into some difficulties along the course of our *Spiritual Timeline* and found ourselves trapped within material *Universes* of our own collaborative *creation*.

Since we did not start out our existence in a trapped condition, it is correct to say that we have *"fallen"* from our native *"godlike"* states. It did not happen all at one, but progressively and systematically. We know our "troubles" have resulted from accumulated "barriers" and "blockages"—or *fragmentation*—during our vast experiences as *Spiritual Beings*. They are not because we lack something; but because of what's been added.

In *Systemology*, we systematically examine those routes by which we must have descended to reach our present condition, then reverse the direction of travel and chart a personal *"Pathway to Ascension."* Of course, the exact "details" of the *Spiritual Timeline* will be different for each individual *Seeker*. However, we have been able to systematically chart our *Pathway* based on common patterns of *Human fragmentation*.

In the most basic terms: the *fragmentation* that defines our "downward spiral" consists of decisions or considerations where we deny our true nature. This includes those decisions to *"withdraw"* rather than *"reach"*; where we choose to *not-know* rather than *know*; to *not-communicate* rather than *communicate*; and ultimately, to take *no-responsibility* for being a *creative-cause*, and therefore succumb to being an *effect*.

But there is *hope!* And much more importantly: there is an effectively workable *way out* of the mazes and traps of our existence. If you are reading this now, you have already begun to gather your tools and build up the *"horsepower"* necessary to break the gravity holding your *Spiritual Beingness* to the *Human Condition.*

STUDYING THE
PROFESSIONAL COURSE

Most *Seekers* study and practice *Systemology* at-a-distance and independent of the "Mardukite Academy" or any "Master-level" mentors trained therein. This means that the *books* (and to a lesser degree, the *internet*) are the only means of direct contact a *Seeker* maintains with the "Systemology Society" during their studies. A continuing *Seeker* from the *"Basic Course"* will be familiar with the style of study found in *this* course.

Misunderstood words are the most common reason an individual abandons studying a subject. When a misunderstanding occurs, *Awareness* declines. These misunderstandings start to "stack up" after the first occurrence, and as a result, the level of interest and attention will also decline. This is how a "confusion" develops; and the individual will get "bored" with the subject, feel tired, and unable to concentrate.

One solution is to return to the part of the material that was still interesting and enjoyable to read. When scanning around that area of text, there is likely to be a new word (or new specific use of a familiar word) that is unclear, but was passed by unnoticed. All *Systemology* books include their own *glossary*. Using this *glossary* and a high-quality dictionary will help resolve this misunderstanding once it is located.

An effective education of any subject is taught on a *gradient*. This is what is intended by presenting the study of something as "*grades*." Rather than treating a subject as one total mass, true learning is achieved by increasing one's understanding with a *gradual* increase upward. The *ascent* to a mountaintop is not successfully achieved in one leap, but by targeting and reaching specific checkpoints along the way.

This *Professional Course* consists of a series of lessons (booklets) that gradually increase a *Seeker's* ability to understand and apply the practices and techniques of *Systemology* as a complete "*Pathway to Ascension.*" It is an appropriate study for continuing *Seekers* (from the *Basic Course*), but also "advanced" *Systemologists*.

Each lesson (booklet) of the *Professional Course* applies *Systemology* to a particular subject (or focus). It is best if the entire course can be studied and applied in sequential order. These lessons also employ a style of practice or technique called *"Systematic Processing."* An introduction to applying this methodology is provided in the final lesson (booklet) of the *Basic Course*—or in the *"Fundamentals of Systemology"* volume.

To study the *Professional Course* just like a student at the Academy: a *Seeker* reads through all instructional material and applies each exercise (or *"process"*) presented in the text to the extent they comfortably can, before continuing on to the next lesson (booklet).

When first starting on the *Pathway* as a *Solo* practitioner, without the aid of an experienced *Pilot*, a *Seeker* shouldn't "push too hard" or allow themselves to get too "stuck" on any one area (lesson) or *process*. It is not expected that any one area will be completely handled when first introduced. For optimum results, it is expected that a serious *Seeker* will make more than one "pass" through the entire *Professional Course.*

The *Professional Course* is not altogether different from other forms of practical or technical education: where the instruction and exercises are delivered to a completion, and then a student further increases their abilities, strength and skill-level by applying additional practice throughout their life. Therefore, a student should not concern themselves with perfectly mastering each step (or lesson) before progressing forward.

Additional passes through the material are likely to result in different "*realizations*" (an increased *level of understanding*) than a previous time. New "layers" of *Knowingness* may now be accessible during a *process* that may not have been before. It is important to avoid invalidating the progress you've made just because one area is not completely handled right away, or if a certain *process* seems too difficult on the first pass.

CHARTING A COURSE ON THE PATHWAY

Although we can communicate a systematic structure to *fragmentation*, the personal journey experienced along the *Pathway* will be different for each *Seeker*. For example, certain areas will seem more "*turbulent*" or difficult for one *Seeker* than another. We tend to say that these areas have more "*charge*" on them—or that they are more "*heavily charged*." It is best to handle such areas when you are already feeling "good" and not in a situation (or condition) where that specific area is consistently being "*triggered*" or "*restimulated*."

As an applied philosophy, *Systemology* "theory" can be easily utilized in the "laboratory" of the "world-at-large" in everyday life. This is implied within the basic instruction of each lesson. Unlike other "sciences" that conduct experiments by making a change to some "objective variable" *out there* and waiting to see an effect, our focus is the individual (or *Observer*) themselves, and how *they* affect the "*Reality*" perceived.

In addition to applying *Systemology* "New Thought" to everyday life, our philosophy is applied by using specific exercises and systematic techniques. These "*processes*" provide the most stable personal gain (and *realizations*) for each area; but only when actually applied with a *Seeker's* full "*presence*" and *Awareness*.

This *Professional Course* is designed so that it may be easily read and studied with little concern for what "dangers" these teachings—or *processing*—might unleash. However, there are still some guidelines that pertain to the "best-uses" of these course lessons, particularly if a *Seeker* intends for stable development.

Skipping over too much material/*processing* in early lessons may make attempts to understand (or apply) later lessons more difficult. However, once the complete *Professional Course* is worked through at least once in its entirety, specific areas can then be later returned to and treated with a greater sense of *Awareness* and *"presence"* than before. Of course, in *"Traditional Piloting,"* the rate of processing is monitored by an experienced practitioner; but in *"Solo-Processing,"* a *Seeker* must regulate their own progress on the *Pathway*.

Applying a systematic technique is called *"running a process."* The *processes* are designed with very simple instructions or *"command-lines."* To *run* a *processing command-line*, a *Seeker* may be assisted by the communication of that *line* from a *"Co-Pilot"* (as in *"Traditional Piloting"*). But even then, a *Seeker* must still personally "input" the *command* as *Self*. For this reason —and quite thankfully— *Solo-Processing* is possible.

TAKING FLIGHT ON THE PATHWAY

Processing Techniques are intended to treat the *Spiritual Being* or *Alpha-Spirit*; the individual themselves. It is applied by the *Alpha-Spirit*—then *Self-directed* to the "Mind-System" or even a "body" (*genetic-vehicle*), both of which are "constructs" that the *Alpha-Spirit* (*Self*, or the "I-AM" *Awareness unit*) operates, but neither of which is actually *Self*. *Fragmentation* causes *Humans* to falsely identify *Self as* the *"Mind"* or even a *"Body."*

The *Professional Course* lessons (booklets) are designed for the *Beginning Seeker* in mind—one that may have an understanding of theory, but with little experience in practice. That being said: each of these lessons may be used toward total *Beta-Defragmentation* within a specific area. There are also more *processes* given for each subject than may be necessary to achieve an *ultimate end-point realization* on that entire area.

Some *processes* can be treated quite lightly at first; others may require a bit of working at in order to get *"running"* well. It is important to set aside a period of time when you can be dedicated to your studies and *processing*. This period of time is referred to as a *"processing session."* The reason for this, is that when a *process* does start *running* well, it is important to be able to complete it to a satisfactory *"end-point."*

The purpose of *systematic processing* is to be able to *really* "look" at things and even determine the *considerations* we have made—or attitudes we have decided—about *Reality* as a result of those experiences. It doesn't do us much good to simply "glance"—or to *restimulate* something uncomfortable and then quickly *withdraw* from it once again, leaving more of our *attention* yet again behind and held fixedly on it.

Generally speaking, a *Seeker* continues to *run* a *process* so long as something is "happening"—which is to say, the *process* is still producing a change. Usually this is evident by the type of "answers" that a *command-line* helps a *Seeker* originate from the database of their own *Mind-System*. The *command-lines* do not "do" anything on their own. They assist a *Seeker* to direct their own attention toward increasing *Awareness*.

Of course, a *Seeker* may also cease to generate new "data" from a *process* without reaching an *"ultimate" realization* as an *"end-point."* It is possible that additional "layers" (or even other "areas") require handling before anything "deeper" is accessible. If this is the case, end the *process*. But, if a *Seeker* is *withdrawing* from something uncomfortable that was incited or stirred up, then a *process* is *run* until they feel "good" about it.

In case the thought of encountering *"turbulence"* is a concern: the techniques given as *"Opening Procedures"* of a *Formal Session* (in the *Basic Course*), and those found in the earliest lessons of the *Professional Course*, are quite useful when applied as "safety nets" for maintaining *Awareness* and *presence*, even when *Flying-Solo*.

One of the benefits to *Flying-Solo* is that *processing* is entirely *Self-determined*. This already provides a certain built-in "safety" for a practitioner. Anything you *restimulate* by *Self-determinism* is *your thing*. It is not incited by external *other-determined* influences (or other "source-points" in existence) that make you an *effect*. It can be more easily handled in *processing*—or you can simply let things "cool down" and come back to it again.

While it may seem "mysterious" to beginners, a *Seeker* gets a sense for knowing how long to *run* a *process* only with practice. Once you have spent some time actually applying the *Professional Course*, there are many aspects that become "second nature" because they are, in fact, a part of our true original nature. All we have done is "*reverse engineer*" the routes of *creation* and *consideration* that are already *our own*.

LESSON NINE:
CONFRONTING
THE PAST

EXPERIENCING EXISTENCE

This lesson (booklet) begins with some upper-grade philosophy to lead off *Systemology Level-4*. It is rather important for a *Seeker* to have completed *all* previous lessons of this *Professional Course* (and preferably also the *Basic Course* that precedes it) before continuing onward with the *Pathway* from this point.

Throughout this *course*, a *Seeker* has gradually increased their *willingness* (or *tolerance*) for "facing up to," "looking at," or else *"confronting"* various *"things."* Our systematic approach began with peeling away lighter surface "layers" before progressing into "heavier" (more *"turbulent"*) expressions or manifestations of *fragmentation*. The "logic" behind the "sequence" of procedures used on this *Pathway* becomes more apparent as we start handling "deeper"—more *"repressed"*—layers of *unknowingness* and *fragmentation.*

Properly "handling"—or *confronting*—the "past" is treated (or *processed*) no differently than when handling "present" *existence* (or *conditions* thereof). For purposes of *defragmentation*, there really *is no* difference—because a *fragmented* individual, themselves, is not actually handling a proper "distinction" of *"time."* For them: *"past imprinting"* dictates *"present perceptions"* and *"future action."* *Time* becomes entangled altogether.

The inherent nature of *fragmentation* is that it "sticks" an individual's *attention/Awareness* somewhere on their *"Backtrack"* and then "tricks" them into continuously maintaining a *creation* of that *reality* as *"present-time"* well afterward. This continuous (and *Self-propagating*) *creation* (and carrying) of *fragmentat-*

ion causes us to experience *restimulated emotional turbulence, compulsive reaches, reactive withdrawals* — and *entrapment* in *barriers* (and other *considerations* about *reality*) we have *agreed* to, even if we have since forgotten.

In previous *processing levels,* we treated some of what we *"hold-out"* — and *"holdback"* — from expressing toward others; but these types of *"things"* are more readily *known* to us. To proceed further on the *Pathway,* a *Seeker* must also *"uncover"* or *"resurface"* those *"things"* which they even have "hidden" from themselves. So, this is the next area we *systematically* target with *processing.*

CREATION AND EXISTENCE

In *Systemology Level-4,* we restore *Actualized Awareness* and increase a *Seeker's* ability to *confront* (or face a *thing* "As-It-Is") by bringing things into view that the *Seeker*, themself, has "*repressed.*" This is to say: they are "*protesting*" the *existence* of it —attaching *considerations* to "make-*Nothing*-of-it"—even if *unknowingly*.

Various intellectual philosophies have been drawn around a human understanding of "*conditions*" and "*states*" of *Existence*. A continuing student or *Seeker* (from previous lessons) should have little difficulty in understanding and applying our *systematic* approach to this subject; but it is important that this subject *is* understood before attempting to progress further on the *Pathway* (using our *processing* methodology).

We frequently use the phrase "*As-It-Is*" in our *Systemology*. This is not fancy wordplay. We mean it exactly "as-it-is" intended. The truest form of a *creation* is the "thing" *As-It-Is*; exactly *As-It-Is*. The problem with treating "existence," is that an individual is likely to *consider* what *it* "was" (*past*), and "might be," "could be," or "will be" (in the *future*). Still: none of those *figuring-thoughts* and *considerations* are the "thing" *As-It-Is*.

Fragmentation of "*perception*" and "*consideration*" is what prompts *continuous compulsive creation* of the *Physical Universe* (*Beta-Existence*). "*Perpetuation*" and "*continuation*" are *considerations* of *Time*; and it is only when things are consistently "*altered*" and "*changed*" from their original state that they "*continue*" in *Time*.

At this *level*, we are most concerned with how this philosophy applies to *personal defragmentation processing*; meaning, in regards to an individual's own *creation* (and *experience*) of a *Personal Universe* based on the "*impressions*" received from environmental/external "*cues*" (such as "*forms*" and "*bodies*") in *Beta-Existence*.

An individual would not be so entrapped

by the *Human Condition* or participation in *this Physical Universe* if they experienced *Existence "As-It-Is."* When in a state of *Self-Honesty*, the *fragmentation* and *illusion* of the *Physical Universe* is not nearly as "solid" and "restimulative." But, of course, this is not the position that most individuals (as *Alpha-Spirits*) are operating from—thus, *fragmentation* perpetuates and becomes more solid.

The experience of *Existence* from the viewpoint of the *Human Condition* is not a *Self-Honest* experience of *Existence "As-It-Is."* Instead, it is an experience based on that same *Existence* "plus" additional *considerations* and *perceptions* specific to the *Human Condition.* That means "*it is altered*" from its original state in order to be experienced at all from that viewpoint. Rather than "*As-It-Is*," we experience "*It-As-Changed.*"

In terms of *systematic processing,* "*fragmentation*" and "*alteration*" ("*It-Is-Altered*" or "*It-As-Changed*") are essentially synonymous. Entangled and turbulent energy composing *fragmentation* is "suspended in place" (*persists* or is *continuously created*) only because it is an "*alteration*" or "*deviation*" of "*truth*" or "*actuality.*"

The "*reality*" that is *agreed-to* and *experienced* is a "lower class" of existence than what things "*actually*" are. A thing *is* what it *is* because it *is*. Everything beyond that is a *consideration* or *associative-thought* related to other experiences, data, or vocabulary, *&tc.*

For example: a particular title of a book may have many copies in existence and is neither rare nor scarce. However, an individual may choose to "hold on to" a certain copy they have, because of some attached "sentimental" value. Perhaps a beloved family member gave it to them. Its "*IS-factor*" has been "*altered.*" While the *actual* book might be found in every thrift-store in the city (and could theoretically be given away and recovered/created at will), the individual feels *"compelled"* (*compulsion*) to retain their *"changed"* copy.

We are not trying to make a point here that a *Seeker* should give up any "sentiment" on all things. We are simply using this example to illustrate why we retain (and *compulsively create*) our *altered* version of *existence* as personal *fragmentation* —and how easily we can *alter* our personal *reality (experience)* of things.

All of our past experiences on the *"Backtrack"* seem so personally unique and significant that we tend to not want to let them go. And most of them do not have a strongly negative effect on us. However, there are also those things that continue to negatively influence our *perceptions*— those things we don't want to "face" or *confront*—which "persist" *unknowingly* because of how far we have *altered* and pushed them "out-of-view."

We have then described *three* primary "*IS-factors*" of *Existence*: there is the true or pure form as originally created or intended "*As-It-Is*"; there are the additions or alterations of "*It-As-Changed*"; and finally, when what is *actually* there is not *confronted*, but is instead *altered* to the point where it is undesirable to "look" at, we *consider* "*It-As-Nothing*" and try to make "*it not exist*" by means of applying additional *energy* and *force.*

This accurately describes the entire *systematic* "sequence" of *repressed* deeply-laden *fragmentation*. Of course, when "*resurfaced*" in *systematic processing (defragmentation)*, the "sequence" is experienced in reverse. When the "*It-As-Nothing*" (and "*Not-Known*") *considerations* are initially lifted, the "*It-As-Changed*" (or "*Almost Known*") and *imprinted considerations* come into view first. These must be *processed* before the true "*As-It-Is*" (or "*Actually Known*") *creation* may exist or not (at will) with full high-power *Alpha-Thought.*

[There are many "upper-level" applications of this philosophy (concerning "*Universes*" or "*objective reality*") that some *Seekers* have had intermittent and sporadic experiences with—which causes them to run astray *before* completing the *Pathway.* Any such "*psychic phenomenon*" (or however you choose to classify it) is really a byproduct of *Beta-Defragmentation* and not a targeted "goal" attached to this *Professional Course.*]

HANDLING EXISTENCE

Fragmentation consisting of "*It-As-Changed*" (*altered*) content is a persistent trouble source that there is at least *some Knowingness* of. But once it is pushed to a level of "*It-As-Nothing*" (*deeply repressed*), it is not only a persistent trouble source, but also entangles potential *Actualized*

Awareness in its *continuous creation* "out-of-sight." It still exists. There was *first* an *Altered Something* to "*protest*" the "existence-of" and *then* an attempt to make *Nothing-Of.* But, it is not *actually* "erased" or "destroyed" *As-It-Is* if treated as something other than *As-It-Is.*

For example: a woman receives jewelry from her lover. For our purposes: she has *imprinting* from *past experiences* that *alters* her perception of this activity. Perhaps a former lover was in the habit of giving her jewelry after having an affair. This produces *reactivity* toward the *past* that is now applied to the *present.*

Instead of having *confronted* the *past imprinting*, perceptions of the present situation are being *altered* with emotionally turbulent "*mental imagery*" of cheating lovers, *&tc.* As this *restimulation* becomes more intrusive and harder to *confront*, more effort (*attention* and *Awareness*) is applied to "push it" further "out of view."

During *systematic processing*, once the *repressed* nature of the *fragmentation* can be lifted, the first *"mental imagery"* that comes into view is the "cheating lover." But this data may not consist of the entire *"chain-of-fragmentation."* It is likely that other similar earlier negative experiences (in the past) also contribute to the consistent *repression* of that area of *fragmentation* when left *not-confronted*. This *deep repression* affects our ability to *confront* (and even properly "remember" or "recall") entire areas of our past (*Backtrack*) As-It-Is.

The *Alpha-Spirit* is essentially a representative of the *Infinity-of-Nothingness*. As a "balancing factor," its native position (or state) consists of the ability to *create* a *Potential Everythingness*.

At our "highest" *god-like* state, we would

want to have *Everything* "available" to us for *creation*—to have the full range of *creating* or *not-creating* things (at will) in *Self-Honesty*. This state requires no *fragmentation* to "unknowingly" or "reactively" influence a *compulsive reach* (*compelled toward*) or *repulsive withdrawal* (*repelled away*) to/from anything. Such *fragmentation* gradually reduces the total "*god-like abilities*" (*Actualized Awareness*) once available to the individual; and *defragmentation* gradually "rehabilitates" these conditions.

We will start off lightly applying this high-level theory and philosophy in practice (for *processing*). For example: an individual might be worried that some undesirable thing might be true, or perhaps something might have been done to them in the past; but in either case, the *uncertainty* produces a *confusion* in that area. This, in itself, generates personal feelings of "*withdrawal*" or "*reluctance to reach*" to some degree.

Now, if this area were *confronted* properly, the *actual truth* would either be *Known*, or at the very least, there would be no reactive reluctance to *"find out."* At higher levels of *Self-Actualization* (*Awareness*), an individual wouldn't necessarily even "care" either way, because it wouldn't persist enough to be troublesome. But, if this can't be achieved *Self-Honestly* by simply "looking at" (or *"confronting"*) something *As-It-Is*, then "deeper" *fragmentation* is present, and inhibiting an experience of *clear perception* (*Knowingness*).

There are many techniques described throughout this *Professional Course* that, once understood and mastered, may then be applied as single applications to particular situations. Most of them are designed to increase one's *ability* and *willingness* to *"confront"* something (or an area) with increased *Awareness*. For example: a *Seeker* could *imagine* various *"mental images"* of a thing happening, *copying* them next to each other many times, until they can be "created," "looked at" and "thrown away" easily.

If supporting lessons (background instruction) on this type of approach (or other techniques) are not readily available (or presently known to the student) consider *running* a *process* this wise on something persistently worrisome or troublesome:

1. *"Recall (or imagine) a time when you did something like this to someone (or caused it to happen to someone)."*
2. *"Recall (or imagine) a time when something like this happened to you (or something like this was true)."*
3. *"Recall (or imagine) a time when someone did something like this (or caused it to happen) to another."*

These *processing command-lines* ("PCL") are alternated repeatedly to "build up" *Awareness* on an area. Using *"recall"* is preferred; but if an actual occurrence cannot be easily *"spotted"* on the *Backtrack*, the *Seeker* can *"imagine"* an appropriate approximation. And this is not to say that the real source of the *basic fragmentation* is not "buried" beneath many layers of, what is likely to be, *"partially imagined data"* anyways. This *process* may be *run* as needed to compliment other related *processes* for a particular area or occurrence.

BASIC PROCESSES

Each one of the following *processes* may only bring something into view, or it may *defragment* the area altogether (on inspection). PCL are run in alternation. They target the *"It-As-Nothing"* level of *consideration*. When a point is reached where the *process* seems complete, or you "feel good" about it, then *end* it. If something "hidden" came into view, but still feels unresolved, then also *run* the previous *process* given above.

PROCESS #1

1A. *"What might you avoid thinking about?"*

1B. *"What don't you have to avoid thinking about?"*

2A. *"What might someone else avoid thinking about?"*

2B. *"What wouldn't someone else avoid thinking about?"*

PROCESS #2

1A. *"What might you pretend never happened?"*

1B. *"What would be acceptable to have happened?"*

2A. *"What might someone else pretend never happened?"*

2B. *"What would someone else find acceptable to have happened?"*

PROCESS #3

1A. *"What might you have made nothing of?"*

1B. *"What wouldn't you need to make nothing of?"*

2A. *"What might someone else have made nothing of?"*

2B. *"What wouldn't someone else need to make nothing of?"*

SYSTEMATIC DEFRAGMENTATION

At this point of the *Professional Course* (and the *Pathway*), a *Seeker* will have *run* hundreds of *processes* and mastered dozens of techniques for handling various difficulties of *Human Life*. The *processing methods* given in these course lessons are also supplemented with an education of our unique *systemological philosophies*.

As a *Seeker* applies *processing* to different areas of their life, some of them will untangle and unravel—or *defragment*—areas sufficiently enough to "fall away" and cease to affect them altogether. There will be others that are more deeply *fragmented* —producing greater *turbulence*—and the *processes* already given may only "soften" them enough to be more manageable (in *processing* and *everyday life*), but they continue to get "*restimulated*."

It requires increased *Actualized Awareness* (and an ability to *confront*) for one to *actually see* how *Self* is "tricked" into essentially *creating* and *solidifying* its own *entrapment*. It is far easier to pass this *responsibility* or *cause* onto some "other-determined" *Source*—but by doing so, we "mask" or "disguise" (*alter*) the *truth*, and therefore relinquish the *control* necessary (and due to us) to properly handle and manage our *creations*.

The *processing* regimen (and lessons)

provided in the *Professional Course* introduces all areas of our *Systemology* with an aim at *"Beta-Defragmentation"* —meaning a handling of *this lifetime*. But, of course, the underlying reasons, mechanics and *considerations* that lead to *"Human Problems,"* and troublesome areas of life, stretch back on a *"chain-of-fragmentation"* extending to many *lifetimes* in many *universes*.

For example: a *Seeker* that is able to master the training and *processing* of *Lesson-4* should be able to take apart (and handle) the "anatomy" of *Human Problems* sufficiently enough to experience some relief. But, of course, many of the *earliest* "problems" we experienced on the *Backtrack*— knowingly as *"god-like" Alpha-Spirits*—are still with us, influencing and impinging on the manifestation of *Existence* that we experience everyday.

There are many areas of our life that have *fragmented energetic-charge* attached to them—entangled personal *energy* and *Awareness* that is "wound up," and just waiting to "spring" (manifest) upon "activation" or *restimulation*. If you have been progressing well on the *Pathway* up to this point, then you have likely experienced some significant *"release points"* and *"end realizations"* along the way. These help increase *certainty* and personal *confidence*, in addition to heightened *Awareness* and ability to *discharge* the *fragmentation* that is *restimulated* by the general experience of everyday life.

Of course, *processing* on the *Pathway* is not "fool-proof." There are times, particularly when *Flying-Solo* (and without additional aids, such as a *"biofeedback device"*) that a *Seeker* may find difficulties or overwhelming *turbulence*. This *Professional Course* was designed to apply to the largest number of potential *Seekers*, thus our emphasis has been on *Solo-Processing* techniques that are effective in *"destimul-*

ating" fragmentation, even in the presence of a "heavy" *charge*.

More often than not, we are intentionally *"resurfacing"* or *"restimulating"* a specific thing in *processing* in order to *"discharge"* (and *defragment*) the *turbulence* (and *fragmented considerations*) directly. We do this *knowingly* and *systematically* to handle with *processing* what would otherwise be *restimulated* by other-determined *sources* and simply build-up as additional *fragmentation*.

To be effective, these *higher processing levels* (that our *Professional Course* now approaches on the *Pathway*) require that a *Seeker* have already reached a certain point of "relief and release" from previous *levels*. It is important to have the *confidence* and *ability* to "cool down" *turbulent upsets* when they are *restimulated* before directing *processing* toward *fragmentation mechanisms* on a more general basis. In brief: you deal with what is already happening, restimulated, or available, before you go digging around deeper for more.

The best course of action in maintaining progress and earning stable results is to practice "preventative" applications of *Systemology*. This means handling the key areas—or *"hot buttons"*—that contribute to accumulating *fragmentation* during everyday *Human* experiences. The *fragmentary dust* of these "normal" *upsets* may be "brushed off" before accumulating into an overwhelming *charge*.

At this time we will identify some *"hot buttons"* from former lessons. As *upper-level* applications, they serve as "preventative fundamentals" to handling everyday life as a more *Self-Actualized* individual—but also to ensure greater effectiveness of *upper-level processing*. Should any of these *"hot buttons"* be actively "pressed" or affecting a *Seeker*, then additional progress on the *Pathway* slows or stalls completely.

PREVENTATIVE FUNDAMENTALS

There are three key *"hot buttons"* that are most troublesome to a *Seeker* (*processing* their way along the *Pathway*) if they are ignored rather than handled (or *confronted*). The primary handling of these areas is covered in former lessons of this *Professional Course*; but by illuminating them here together, we can discuss their application as "preventative fundamentals" for everyday life and *upper-level processing*. They are:

1. A *break* or *upset* in the "*Flow-Factors*" — enforced or inhibited *communication, likingness* and/or *agreement*. [see *Lesson-7, "Eliminating Barriers"*]

2. A "*Human Problem*" — present-time *attention* (*presence*) is occupied fixedly else

where (and outside one's own control). [see *Lesson-4, "Handling Humanity"*]

3. A "*Hold-Out*" —*attention* restimulated the area, usually because someone else *almost found out* about it. [see *Lesson-6, "Escaping Spirit-Traps"*]

In *Traditional Processing*, a *Professional Pilot* would usually check these "*hot buttons*" at the beginning of a *Formal Session*. This rudimentary step has obviously required additional training (to employ effectively in *processing*) and is not included in the basic *Formal Session Script* given as an example at the very start of the course. Some *Seekers* even make a practice of checking for these "*buttons*" in a daily *session*.

You might check these over now, at this point of the lesson, and see if there is anything present that requires handling. Usually, a *Solo-Pilot* does not have to check these over at every *session* if they are *processing* often and moving along the

Pathway well. If something does come up in life, you will usually be able to recognize it and handle it—but, of course, in *Traditional Processing* (*Co-Piloted*), a *Professional* would check these over each time just to ensure the best results possible from the remainder of the *session*.

As a general rule: if a *Seeker's attention* is presently "stuck" or "fixed" on one of these *"buttons"*—an *upset*, *problem* or *holdout*—then additional *"subjective"* *processing* techniques are not going to be effective unless they are targeting that area directly. On the other hand, *"objective"* techniques (involving *selectively directing attention* on *objects/environment*) can often aid in "cooling down" enough to allow for *subjective processing*.

For example: you can apply the *preventative fundamentals* to help "clean up" something that just happened in regards to one of the areas targeted by the former lessons of this *Professional Course*. Each lesson addresses specific areas and usually includes a general technique that may be adapted for "single-use" handling of a specific thing that has just been "stirred up" or manifested as a "barrier" of some kind.

Usually, when an area has been completely *run* to a stable "*release-point*," a *Seeker* is mostly free from *fragmentation* in that area—so, when something related does come up, they are able to simply *confront* it (and apply knowledge of that area) to the situation to *prevent* any persistent issues. Of course, if a *Seeker* finds their *attention* fixed on some troublesome area, then a review of these *fundamentals* may be in order.

Now, eventually, as a *Seeker* begins to handle more and more areas, some of the earlier "*release-points*" will *destabilize*. This is normal—and it occurs because the range of *Awareness* (or *availability* of "*knowables*") is expanding. More of the data from "hidden areas" becomes accessible—and, of course, this means there is much more available to *process* in an area then when having experienced the previous *"release-point."*

For example: during a *Seeker's* first "pass" through the *Professional Course* material, the *processing* on a certain area is *run* to a *"relief"* or *"release-point"* involving what is currently available—and if that technique would be *run* further, it would be *overrun*. However, as a *Seeker* works further and deeper into various areas, when you go through an additional "pass" through the material, there is more available now to *run*—and those earlier *processes* become useful again for progressing further into the various areas.

To advance our example further: supposing we take the area of *"protest"* or *"problems"* for this example; a *Seeker* might first *run* through the material as a basis for stable *Beta-Defragmentation*, using the *viewpoint* of *this* single "*Human*" lifetime for *processing*—and upon completion, will experience a great deal of increased *Awareness* and *Self-Actualization*. But as more of the *Backtrack* comes into view, concerning a long span of existence as an *Alpha-Spirit*, there are much "higher" *viewpoints* that may also be handled further. Having already maintained the first stable point, these more "advanced" areas are more accessibly reached.

In *Traditional Piloting*, if a *Seeker* slows or stalls on the *Pathway*, it is up to the *Pilot* to determine why. Of course, really it is only the *Seeker*, themselves, that knows—even if they don't think that it is the reason why. But, it is still a *Pilot's* responsibility to discover it for all concerned, and often this involves probing various areas directly (often with the assistance of an electronic *biofeedback device*).

In *Solo-Piloting*, a *Seeker* is left to discover underlying *fundamental breaks* or *upsets* themselves—*identifying* and *confronting* them directly.

In addition to targeting the three key *preventative fundamentals*, a *Professional Pilot* will usually "probe" the following list:

—Has anything been *protested*;

—Have you committed a *Harmful-Act*;

—Is anything being *suppressed/repressed*;

—Has there been a *false accusation*;

—Has anything been *invalidated*;

—Has someone *enforced* an *evaluation*;

—Are you *holding-out* a *communication*;

—Has there been a *misunderstanding*.

Somewhere within all of these areas, the underlying reason for slows and stalls will usually be found.

There is one additional aspect that we have not yet covered in this course, mainly because it pertains specifically to *systematic processing* itself, and not one of the typical areas of *fragmentation* (such as with previous lessons). As mentioned briefly earlier: our communication of *Systemology* is not "fool-proof"—and individuals do make mistakes in *processing*. Therefore, *"processing errors"* are the additional reason why a *Seeker* might run into trouble now and then when using our methodology. This makes for an almost unique form of very light *"potential fragmentation"* that is specific only to our own *Seekers*.

Perhaps one of the most frustrating *processing errors* is "looking for something that isn't there." There may be a previous mistake or misunderstanding that leads to it; but for whatever reason, a *Seeker* may decide that something is "there" or "true" when it isn't. For example: deciding that there is a *break* in a *Flow-Factor* when there really isn't, so *running* that for "relief" turns out to make them feel more *confused* or *upset* than before—because obviously that wasn't *it*, *&tc*. This generates greater *turbulence* than should be there.

Processing Errors are not the "end of the world." If you can simply "*spot*" the point where you went wrong, or got a "*wrong indication*" from a *process* or exercise, then you can "back up" and try again. This can happen even to the most expert among us. All available data or reasoning will *indicate* that one thing or another *is it*, but then once that is done or handled, the original issue seems to remain. This occurs all the time in our everyday world, especially when attempting to "repair" a complex "*machine*" or *system*.

CONFRONTING THE PAST

Individuals tend to *reactively withdraw* from painful and undesirable experiences —and any *associated data* and "*mental imagery*" attached to them. Failing to face—

or *confront*—the contents of an *incident*, an *Alpha-Spirit* stores *fragmented* and *irrational* data regarding the *facets* and *factors* therein.

Defragmenting an *incident* properly using *systematic processing* requires all of the experience, knowledge, and *Actualized Awareness* earned from the *first nine lessons* of this *Professional Course*. This ability is, however, the main staple or *end-goal* of *Systemology Level-4*. It also potentially opens up new areas of the *"Backtrack"* (the part of one's *Spiritual Timeline* that is "past") for *processing past-lives* (as that data becomes more available).

Confronting-the-Past is so critical that it represents an entire tier or *processing level*. Hidden within those past "negative experiences" are *considerations* and high-power *Alpha-Thought "postulates"* about what the *Alpha-Spirit* is no longer *willing* to *Be*, do, or have. This *unwillingness* leads to *creating* automatic/reactive *"mental mechanisms"* (*spiritual machines compulsively created* with *personal energy*) to handle these undesirable *facets* and *factors* on a *continuous* and *"unknowing"* basis. This is quite detrimental to a *god-like Spiritual Being.*

"Unconfronted" (*"repressed"* and *"Not-Known"*) areas become *fragmented* "blind-spots" for the individual. This is, for example, why an individual tends to find themselves in certain circumstances again and again. By not *confronting* it properly —or seeing it *"As-It-Is"*—the effective actions to appropriately handle the situation are not taken. *Reactive withdrawal* (based on earlier *imprinting*) *fragments* one's *clear perception* when it seems like the undesirable thing might happen again—or even when an *associated facet* of it is present.

In *Systemology*, we often use the word *"restimulated"* to describe the *present-time* "activation" of past *fragmentation*. By this, we mean when the circumstances of ordinary life "stir up" or "bring to the surface" the *fragmentation* of past incidents—and, of course, this occurs *outside* or *apart* from the *Self-determinism* of the individual; it happens automatically or reactively. The individual tends to bring the whole past *incident* into the *present*, and often feels (or gets a sense of) the effects of that *incident* as if it has just happened again.

While some of our *vocabulary* and *theory* is specific to *Systemology*, this phenomenon we are describing, has been known to humanity for thousands of years. [Described in the *Systemology Core* volume: "*The Tablets of Destiny Revelation.*"] It is observable in practice; not simply a theoretical idea. Our words, like *imprints*, and explanation of a *Backtrack, are*, however theoretical constructs—but they are workable. Using our ideas provides a greater understanding and more effective results for an individual *Seeker* than the "figuring-thoughts" collected over thousands of years on various types of *spiritual mysticism* and *psychotherapies*.

Our *Systemology* also requires a greater level of *Actualized Awareness* (and personal *realizations*) in order to "go all the way" with it. It requires *Knowing* things with *certainty* that are not so easily accepted when simply "taught" or "instructed." This is why we encourage *Seekers* to actually "apply the work to their life" and not simply treat this as a purely "intellectual philosophy" or "faith-based religion."

For example: the basic underlying *truth* is that the *Alpha-Spirit*—the individual, themselves—*creates* their own *Universe*, their own *mental* and *emotional states*, their own *automated-mechanisms*, and beyond this, even carries around an entire library of painful and undesirable *mental images* that requires suspending *attention* (and *creative ability*) on the *past* in order to hold onto them. Of course, most of this now operates *unknowingly*—however, our complete *Beta-Defragmentation* procedural regimen (as outlined in the *Professional Course*) is designed to bring various areas *knowingly* back under the *control* of the *Seeker*.

It is that "library of old pictures" that we are most concerned with when "*confronting-the-past.*" Essentially, the effects of these *mental images* only linger because they are of things that have not been *confronted.* This is the only reason for an *Alpha-Spirit* to keep them around *compulsively* and *continuously*, rather than just *Knowing* them and being able to "*create*" and "*destroy*" the *mental imagery* at will.

The *Alpha-Spirit* carries *pictures* of *incidents* that have not been properly *confronted.* Since the individual did not fully "face" the *pain* (or *loss*) of what happened, there is now a lack of data (and *Awareness*) in that area. Yet, at the same time, the individual doesn't want it to happen again. This puts them in a position where they are afraid to actually "forget" what happened, but at the same time, still doesn't want to have to deal with it *knowingly.* This is how *fragmentation* can form: *continuously creating* a *reactive mental image* that is allowed to operate without *knowingly* "looking at" or *controlling* it.

Our earliest *systematic* approaches to this phenomenon were (and are) effective, but incomplete. Those *Seekers* using the information in the first edition of *"The Tablets of Destiny"* in exclusion (without the *"Crystal Clear"* companion volume) tended to focus too much attention on vigorously *erasing* the *"pencil lines"* of *fragmentation* (metaphorically speaking) to the point of nearly tearing the "paper."

The more recently developed *upper-grade* approach emphasizes increasing one's *ability* to simply *confront* the past *incidents* to a point where they are no longer inhibiting or affecting present/future *considerations* and *action/creation*; the *"pencil mark"* is no longer "vivid" or "bold" enough to affect whatever else we might do with the page. It is still kind of there, the *incident did really* happen, but we don't care.

True *"Beta-Defragmentation"* occurs when a *Seeker* works with this material long enough to where they no longer need—and therefore can "toss out" or "cease creating"—whatever *mental machinery* they have set up as *Alpha-Spirits* to handle undesirable data. A *"Self-Honest"* individual is no longer *unknowingly compulsively creating* a "library of old painful pictures" that are *reacting* outside one's own *control* and *Self-Determinism.* Of course, this itself is not the *"ultimate"* state of *Ascension* that we refer to—but it is a *necessary prerequisite state* for *Ascension.*

DEFRAGMENTING THE PAST

Whether we call it *Beta-Defragmentation* or *Self-Honesty*, this state we are describing is the first stable point of *"metahumanism"* available to a *Seeker* on the *Pathway*. By this, we mean that it *exceeds* the limited range or parameters that we otherwise use to define the *"Human Condition."* An individual who is free from operating *re-actively* based on *past imprinting* is no longer a *standard-issue "Human."*

Our *systematic* approach works on a *gradual-gradient* to *reach* this state. A *Seeker* simply begins with lighter— easier to *confront—incidents* before *processing* the more difficult ones. Doing this allows a *Seeker* to *gradually* increase their *Actualized Awareness* and *ability-to-confront* the nature of *Existence "As-It-Is"* until greater, older, and deeper areas of one's *past* come into view for inspection (*analytical recall*).

There is also no reason to become overly concerned with searching out *"The (Ultimate) Incident"*—some single instance or *incident* that might be used to explain *all* of a *Seeker's* underlying *fragmentation*. While it is true that there are some *incidents* on the *Backtrack* that have been more detrimental to one's spiritual decline than others, that type of pursuit is not nearly as effective for a *Seeker* (in terms of stable results) as what we present for the *Professional Course*.

Although there are *systematic* guidelines that we follow, there is not only one single way of which to *run* a *process* for *Confronting-the-Past*. In fact, this is one of those practices that we have found evidence of in many times and cultures throughout history. The difference is our *systematic processing methodology*. And for our present purposes, this course will emphasize a technique that is appropriate for *Solo-Piloting*. While *running past incidents* is sometimes handled earlier in practice with *Traditional Piloting*, *Seekers* must have raised their own *Awareness* with *all* former *processing levels* (from previous lessons) before *Flying-Solo* in this area.

The data for these first *processing steps* should be recorded in your *notebook* (or *"flight log"*).

A. *"Identify the incident."*

Simply *"spot"* the *incident* on your *track* (*past*) and identify it with a label. To begin with something simple and presumably *non-restimulative*: we'll use the example of *"getting the mail yesterday"* for our lesson.

B. *"Spot when the incident occurred."*

If you can't *"spot"* the *timing* directly, determine it as closely as you can. Consider ranges of time and see what feels correct. If it happened a long time ago, sometimes it is easier to consider it in terms of its order-of-magnitude—such as how many "years" or "decades" it's been. Be as concise as possible with these *steps*, because it will contribute to how clearly you can bring an *incident* into view *"As-It-Is."* For our example: you might *spot* the *"exact time that you started walking to the mailbox."*

C. *"Spot the duration of the incident."*

Determine "how long" (time-frame) the *incident* lasted. This helps improve *recall* accuracy. For our example: we might *spot* a *"ten second duration of walking to the mailbox."*

D. *"Spot the location of the incident."*

Determine exactly "where" the *incident* took place. At the very least (for older or more obscure *incidents*), try to get a sense of the "direction" and "distance" it was from your present location. In our basic example: we might have *spotted* the *"location of the mailbox."*

E. *"Spot the size-of-space that the incident took place in."*

This helps provide a background for which the *incident* will be viewed. Did it take place in a large space outdoors or a small room or did it happen across many miles, *&tc.* For our example: we *spot* the *"spatial area of the yard between the front door and the mailbox; a walked path of approximately 100 feet."*

F. *"Close your eyes."*

This obviously completes the preliminary *"written"* *steps* of the *process.*

G. *"Move to the beginning of the incident."*

Direct your *attention* to the *actual* time when the *incident* happened. *Recreate* the *"beginning"* point of your experience of the *incident* as if the scenery is all around you—as if you were actually there again. In our example: one might *spot "standing at the front door looking out across the yard at the mailbox."*

H. *"Move through the incident."*

Do your best to completely *re-experience* the *incident*. See what you can *notice* or *perceive* about everything that happened in it.

I. *"Open your eyes; write down what happened, what you noticed or perceived."*

Record everything that happened and anything you perceived. This is done to see it as "external" and "separate" from *Self.* For our example: we might record that we *"walked across the yard, reached the mailbox, opened it, and found it empty."* Other perceptions (things noticed) might include the "weather," "smells," if any "animals" were present, *&tc.*

J. [*Repeat Steps F through I.*]

Run through the *incident* again. When you get to the "written" part, simply record any *new* details that may have been noticed this time.

After *running* the *incident* a couple times, a *Seeker* should be able to tell if the *fragmented charge* associated with the *incident* is being "*processed out,*" or if it is getting more "*solid*" and difficult to *confront.*

If the *fragmented charge* is being properly "*processed out,*" then some *new* details *should* emerge that you didn't notice on the first *run*—or some of the details might "rearrange" themselves to be more in line with *truth.* In either case, the actual "impact" of the *incident* should begin to weaken; it now seems unimportant.

If, however, the *incident* seems like it is getting more "*solid,*" "*heavier*" or more difficult to *run*—as in the act of *confronting* the contents is making you feel worse about it—then there is *earlier* data (such as from a *prior incident*, or even an earlier "beginning point" of the same *incident*) that needs to be *run*.

Our *"mailbox"* example is not very *restimulative* of *fragmentation*; but if it were, and if we were having a hard time of it, then we would look for either an earlier "beginning point" of that *incident*, or an earlier *incident* that also included a *"mailbox"* or *"going to get the mail."* Perhaps the real "beginning" of the *incident* was the *"decision to go out to get the mail, while still inside"* and not *"standing outside the front door."* This would change the *spatial area*, *duration* and other data required to properly *run the incident*.

As you *confront* an *incident* from the past using *systematic processing*, it should become easier. If that is not happening, and you cannot find an earlier beginning-point of the *incident*, then simply "looking at" or "stirring up" this *incident* has actually *restimulated* earlier and deeper *fragmentation*. The only solution is to *spot* or *identify* the earlier one. This happens quite often *unknowingly* in our everyday encounters.

Since an *earlier incident* is being *restimulated*, its virtual presence is usually right there almost "behind" the *incident* you are looking at. If it doesn't come into view right away, usually you can get some sense, feeling, or impression, about it. It is even possibly something more obscure, such as from an *earlier lifetime*. When just starting on *Systemology Level-4*, the only reason to *run incidents* from *past-lives* is if it comes up while *processing your present life*. Whenever you find an earlier "beginning-point" or *incident*, start with "*Step-A*."

"STEP-K" : DEFRAGMENTATION

It is important to note that *heavily charged*

fragmentation has a tendency to *"alter"* and *"change"* the apparent *"IS-*factor" of an *incident*. We call it *"fragmentation"* for a reason; and it has a tendency to *distort* the data that is *recalled* or *considered* when viewing (or attempting to *confront*) a strongly *charged* or *fragmented* *"imprint"* (or *"mental image"* of a past experience). [This is why we covered the nature of *Existence* for the first half of this lesson.]

If the *content* or *sequence-of-events* keeps shifting around, you are still dealing with *"It-As-Changed."* This means you should keep *running* it until the data seems to settle one way or another. Although the general rule is to *run* whatever comes up in *processing*, the data being perceived may be quite inaccurate while the area is still *"heavily charged."* If an individual is still encountering an *incident* *"As-Changed,"* it cannot be properly *confronted* *"As-It-Is."*

You are finished with this *process* when

the *incident* (or *earlier incident*) is completely *"processed-out."* This means there is no longer a *"mental charge"* or *"emotional turbulence"* attached to the *incident* (or *thoughts* and *considerations* of the *incident*). The event, itself, is not actually "forgotten" or "erased from memory." The *mental imagery* can still be *recreated* and *dissolved* at will—but the key here is "at will." There is no longer a reason for the individual to continue *unknowingly compulsively creating* it as *reactive-fragmentation*.

For example: if our personal survival were dependent on the information found in books, than an individual would only compulsively carry around those physical copies of books that they did not already *Know*. If the material were memorized (or *Known*), there would be no need to refer to the book—and no reason to insist on keeping that book close. If, however, the contents of one of them were of such a nature or magnitude that the person could not fully *confront* or truly *Know* it, then they would want to have it as a future reference. This may be a bit on the fantastical side as an example, but it is relevant for our purposes.

The increased *Awareness* and new *realizations* are the *systemological* version of *Knowingness* from this example above. As more areas can be brought up to the level of *Known*, more freedom and clarity is to be had by the individual. The *Alpha-Spirit* is able to regain more *Awareness* and *control* over its own *automated-mechanisms* and the *fragmentation* they have generated. More *Awareness* is available because less "units" of *spiritual attention-energy* are being suspended in the *compulsive continuous creation* of *fragmentation.*

As a *Seeker* progresses further on the *Pathway*, it is possible to get nearly instantaneous *defragmentation* simply by actually *looking* and *confronting* with high-power *Actualized Awareness.* The *Seeker* feels the "relief" just on proper inspection of the *fragmentation.* But more often than not, a *Seeker* will have to repeatedly *run* an *incident* completely through and *spot* whatever they can *notice* about it several times before true *defragmentation* occurs.

Once a *Seeker* reaches an *end-point* on the *processing* as given, the final (more advanced) step of the *defragmentation* procedure is to "*spot any considerations or decisions that were made at the time of the incident.*" This means to actually *identify* the *Alpha-Thought/postulates* that you have carried along ever since—and which are likely to have *unknowingly* influenced the manner in which you experienced *reality* thereafter. This may be too far of a reach on your first pass through this course, but it is an important part of its mastery.

If *Solo-Piloting*, it is better to work with "*uncharged*" *incidents* until you are well-practiced in this technique. Then you can work up to actual *"pain incidents,"* but starting with the more trivial ones, like *"stubbing your toe."* In such an example as the *"mailbox"* or *"stubbing a toe,"* there is likely to be many, many occurrences of a *similar incident.* You don't actually have to work backwards one-by-one with each time. You try to *spot* the *earliest incident* available for *recall*; and then in *running* that, you may discover a new *"earliest"* one. This can happen several times as you gradually increase your *ability-to-confront* for that entire area.

The random aches and pains of life usually stem from, or are more intense because of, *restimulation* of an *earlier incident.* Rather than handling or *processing* a "condition," this technique may be applied to *incidents.* A *Seeker* doesn't use *systematic processing* to *run* "an aching toe," but instead, "impacts to the toe." *Running* a simple pain might even bring you to *confront* a major "accident" or "event," in which case, you handle it as an *incident* with the full procedure given in this lesson.

The "heaviest" *imprint fragmentation* actually developed within *this present lifetime*, will be during periods of "*biological unconsciousness.*" This area is very closely tied to *accidents, physical trauma*, and *medical operations*. It is also tied to very deep far-running *chains-of-fragmentation* that are likely to extend far beyond *this* life. Improving your *Awareness* and *ability-to-confront* any area will bring more into view; just be patient with it, don't push too hard, and this technique might just surprise you.

ON HANDLING "LOSS"

In the beginning, an *Alpha-Spirit* is quite *god-like* in its *creative ability*. Eventually, the lack of *"value,"* with things being so easily *created* and *destroyed*, becomes rather boring. When something *can* be *created* into "infinity," there is nothing to make "this" more valuable or interesting than "that" until we begin to assign *"significances"* to things. So, *"uniqueness"* enters in as a *consideration.*

"Loss" emerges much earlier, further back, on our personal *track* than the idea of "pain" (as a source of potential *fragmentation*). "Pain" is really a *reactive-mechanism* that developed afterward to give warning of a "potential loss." In the case of a *"Human Body,"* the *Alpha-Spirit* has forgotten its own *creative ability* and is dependent on the "body" (failing to be able to *recreate* one at will) and thus there are many *reactive-mechanisms* in place to "protect" against its "loss." But, keep in mind, the *Alpha-Spirit* is still *unknowingly creating* these *mechanisms* too.

On additional, more advanced, "passes" through this course material, you can see just how far the technique can go. For example: you can *run "past-deaths"* from the *viewpoint* of *Self as an Alpha-Spirit,* and *confront* the *loss* of "bodies." This starts to open up wider *considerations* (and *Awareness*) of the *Backtrack* prior to *this* lifetime. You can also *process-out* the *loss* of former civilizations, and even earlier *Universes,* that you once experienced.

You may discover many other potential applications for the *systematic processing* of this *Professional Course* that will assist you in *"reaching further."*

Your only limit is Infinity.

The Systemology Professional Course
continues in the next lesson booklet:
LIFTING THE VEILS

GLOSSARY

actualization : to make actual, not just potential; to bring into full solid Reality; to realize fully in *Awareness* as a "thing."

agreement (reality) : unanimity of opinion of what is "thought" to be known; an accepted arrangement of how things are; things we consider as "real" or as an "is" of "reality"; a consensus of what is real as made by standard-issue (common) participants; what an individual contributes to or accepts as "real"; in *Systemology*, a synonym for "*reality.*"

alpha : the first, primary, basic, superior or beginning of some form; in *Systemology*, referring to the state of existence operating on spiritual archetypes and postulates, will and intention "exterior" to the low-level condensation and solidarity of energy and matter as the 'physical universe' (*beta*).

alpha-spirit : a "spiritual" *Life*-form; the "true" *Self* or I-AM; the *individual*; the spiritual (*alpha*) *Self* that is animating the (*beta*) physical body or "*genetic vehicle*" using a continuous *Lifeline* of spiritual ("*ZU*") energy; an individual spiritual (*alpha*) entity possessing no physical mass or measurable waveform (motion) in the Physical Universe as itself, so it animates the (*beta*) physical body or "*genetic vehicle*" as a catalyst to experience *Self*-determined causality in effect within the *Physical Universe*; a singular unit or point of *Spiritual Awareness* that is *Aware* that it is *Aware.*

alpha thought : the highest spiritual *Self-determination* over creation and existence exercised by an Alpha-Spirit; the Alpha range of pure *Creative Ability* based on direct postulates and considerations of *Beingness*; spiritual qualities comparable to "thought" but originating in Alpha-existence, independently superior to a Mind-System.

ascension : actualized *Awareness* elevated to the point of true "spiritual existence" exterior to *beta existence*. An "Ascended Master" is one who has returned to an incarnation on Earth as an inherently *Enlightened One*, demonstrable in their words and actions; they have the ability to *Self-direct* the "Mind" and "Body" as *Self* (as a "Spirit"); and to maintain consciousness as a personal identity continuum with the same *Self-directed* control and communication of Will-Intention that is exercised, actualized and developed deliberately during one's present incarnation.

associative knowledge : significance or meaning of a facet or aspect assigned to (or considered to have) a direct relationship with another facet; to connect or relate ideas or facets of existence with one another; in traditional systems logic, an equivalency of significance or meaning between facets or sets that are grouped together, such as in $(a + b) + c = a + (b + c)$; in Systemology, erroneous associative knowledge is assignment of the same value to all facets or parts considered as related (even when they are not actually so), such as in $a = a$, $b = a$, $c = a$ and so forth without distinction.

attention : active use of *Awareness* toward a specific aspect or thing; the act of "attending" with the presence of *Self*; a direction of focus or concentration of *Awareness* along a particular channel or conduit or toward a particular terminal node or communication termination point; the Self-directed concentration of personal energy as a combination of observation, thought-waves and consideration; focused application of *Self-Directed Awareness*.

awareness : the highest sense of-and-as *Self* in knowing and being as I-AM (the *Alpha-Spirit*); the extent of beingness directed as a viewpoint (POV) experienced by *Self* as *Knowingness*.

beta (existence) : all manifestation in the "Physical Universe" (KI, in *Zuism*); the conditions of *Awareness* for the *Alpha-spirit* (*Self*) as a physical organic *Lifeform* or "*genetic vehicle*" in which it experiences causality in the *Physical Universe*.

charge : to fill or furnish with a quality; to supply with energy; to lay a command upon; in *Systemology*—to imbue with intention; to overspread with emotion; personal energy stores and significances entwined as fragmentation in mental images, reactive-response encoding and intellectual (and/or) programmed beliefs.

circuit : a circular path or loop; a closed-path within a system that allows a flow; a pattern or action or wave movement that follows a specific route or potential path only; in *Systemology*, "*communication processing*" pertaining to a specific *flow* of energy or information along a channel; "*feedback loop*."

communication : successful transmission of information, data, energy (&tc.) along a message line, with a reception of feedback; an energetic flow of intention to cause an effect (or duplication) at a distance; the personal energy moved or acted upon by will or else 'selective directed attention'; the 'messenger action' used to transmit and receive energy across a medium; also relay of energy, a message or signal—or even locating a personal POV (viewpoint) for the Self—along the *ZU-line*.

confront : to come around in front of; to be in the presence of; to stand in front of, or in the face of; to meet "face-to-face" or "face-up-to"; additionally, in *Systemology*, to fully tolerate or acceptably withstand an encounter with a particular manifestation without an automatic reactive response..

consideration : careful analytical reflection of all aspects; deliberation; determining the significance of a "thing" in relation to similarity or dissimilarity to other "things"; evaluation of facts and importance of certain facts; thorough examination of all aspects related to, or important for, making a decision; the analysis of consequences and estimation of significance when making decisions; also in *Systemology*, the *postulate* or *Alpha-Thought* that defines the state of *beingness* for what something "*is.*"

defragmentation : the *reparation* of wholeness; collecting all dispersed parts to reform an original whole; a process of removing "*fragmentation*" in data or knowledge to provide a clear understanding; applying techniques and processes that promote a *holistic* interconnected *al-*

pha state, favoring observational *Awareness* of continuity in all spiritual and physical systems; in *Systemology*, a "*Seeker*" achieving actualized "*Self-Honest Awareness*" is said to be in a basic state of *beta-defragmentation*, whereas *Alpha-defragmentation* is the rehabilitation of the *creative ability*, managing the *Spiritual Timeline* and the POV of *Self* as Alpha-Spirit (I-AM).

fragmentation : breaking into parts and scattering the pieces; the *fractioning* of wholeness or the *fracture* of a holistic interconnected *alpha* state, favoring observational *Awareness* of perceived connectivity between parts; *discontinuity*; separation of a totality into parts; in *Systemology*, a person outside of *Self-Honesty* is said to be operating from a *fragmented* state.

flow : movement across (or through) a channel (or conduit); a direction of active energetic motion, typically distinguished as either an *in-flow*, *out-flow* or *cross-flow*.

genetic-vehicle : a physical *Life*-form; the physical (*beta*) body that is animated/controlled by the (*Alpha*) Spirit using a continuous *Spiritual Lifeline* (ZU); a physical (*beta*) organic receptacle and catalyst for the (*Alpha*) *Self* to operate "causes" and experience "effects" within the *Physical Universe*.

harmful-act : a counter-survival mode of behavior or action (esp. that causes harm to one of more *Spheres of Existence*)—or—an overtly aggressive (hostile and/or destructive) action against an individual or any other *Sphere of Existence*; in *Utilitarian Systemology*—a short-sighted (serves fewest/lowest *Spheres of Existence*) intentional overtly harmful action to resolve a perceived problem; a revision of the rule for standard *Utilitarianism* for Systemology to distinguish actions which provide the least benefit to the least number of *Spheres of Existence*, or else the greatest harm to the greatest number of *Spheres of Existence*; in *moral philosophy*—an action which can be experienced by few and/or which one would not be willing to experience for themselves (*theft, slander, rape, &tc*); an iniquity or iniquitous act.

hold-back : withheld communications (esp. actions) such as "*Hold-Outs*"; intentional (or automatic) withdrawal (as opposed to reach); Self-restraint (which may eventually be enforced or automated); not reaching, acting or expressing, when one should be; an ability that is now re-strained (on automatic) due to inability to withhold it on Self-determinism alone.

hold-outs : in photography, the numerous snap-shots/pictures withheld from the final display or professional presentation of the event; withheld communications; in Utilitarian Systemology—energetic withdrawal and communication breaks with a "*terminal*" and its *Sphere of Existence* as a result of a "*Harmful-Act*"; unspoken or undiscovered (hidden, covert) actions that an individual withholds communications of, fearing punishment or endangerment of *Self-preservation* (*First Sphere*); the act of hiding (or keeping hidden) the truth of a "*Harmful-Act*"; a refusal to communicate with a *Pilot*; also "*Hold-Back.*"

holistic : the examination of interconnected systems as encompassing something greater than the *sum* of their "parts."

Human Condition : a standard default state of Human experience that is generally accepted to be the extent of its potential identity (*beingness*) —currently treated as *Homo Sapiens Sapiens,* but which is scheduled for replacement by *Homo Novus* (the "New Human").

imprint : to strongly impress, stamp, mark (or outline) onto a softer 'impressible' substance; to mark with pressure onto a surface; in *Systemology*, used to indicate permanent Reality impressions marked by frequencies, energies or interactions experienced during periods of emotional distress, pain, unconsciousness, loss, enforcement, or something antagonistic to physical (personal) survival, all of which are are stored with other reactive response-mechanisms at lower-levels of *Awareness* as opposed to the active memory database and proactive processing center of the Mind; an experiential "memory-set" that may later resurface—be triggered or stimulated artificially—as Reality, of which similar responses will be engaged automatically; holographic-like imagery "stamped" onto consciousness as composed of energetic *facets* tied to the "snap-shot" of an experience.

invalidate : decrease the level or degree or *agreement* as Reality.

pilot : a professional steersman responsible for healthy functional operation of a ship toward a specific destination; in *Systemology*, an intensive trained individual qualified to specially apply *Systemology Processing* to assist other *Seekers* on the *Pathway*.

point-of-view (POV) : a point to view from; an opinion or attitude as expressed from a specific identity-phase; a specific standpoint or vantage-point; a definitive manner of consideration specific to an individual phase or identity; a place or position affording a specific view or vantage; circumstances and programming of an individual that is conducive to a particular response, consideration or belief-set (paradigm); a position (consideration) or place (location) that provides a specific view or perspective (subjective) on experience (of the objective).

postulate : to put forward as truth; to suggest or assume an existence *to be*; to state or affirm the existence of particular conditions; to provide a basis of reasoning and belief; a basic theory accepted as fact; in *Systemology*, Alpha-Thought —the top-most decisions or considerations made by the Alpha-Spirit regarding the "*is-ness*" (what things "are") about energy-matter and space-time.

presence : a quality of some thing (*energy/matter*) being "present" in space-time; personal orientation of *Self* as an *Awareness* (*POV*) located in present space-time (environment) and communicating with extant energy-matter.

processing command line (PCL) or **command line** : a directed input; a specific command using highly selective language for *Systemology Processing*; a predetermined directive statement (cause) intended to focus concentrated attention (effect).

processing, systematic : the inner-workings or "through-put" result of systems; in *Systemology*, a method of applied spiritual technology used toward personal Self-Actualization; methods of selective directed attention, communicated language and associative imagery that increases personal control of the human condition.

realization : the clear perception of an understanding; a consideration or understanding on what is "actual"; to make "real" or give "reality" to so as to grant a property of "being-ness" or "being as it is"; the state or instance of coming to an *Awareness*; in *Systemology*, "gnosis" or true knowledge achieved during *systematic processing*; achievement of a new (or higher) cognition, true knowledge or perception of Self; a consideration of reality or assignment of meaning.

responsibility : the *ability* to *respond*; the extent of mobilizing *power* and *understanding* an individual maintains as *Awareness* to enact *change*; the proactive ability to *Self-direct* and make decisions independent of an outside authority.

Seeker : an individual on the *Pathway to Self-Honesty*; a practitioner of *Mardukite Systemology* or *Systemology Processing*, that is working toward *Spiritual Ascension*.

Self-actualization : bringing the full potential of the Human spirit into Reality; expressing full capabilities and creativeness of the *Alpha-Spirit*.

Self-determinism : the freedom to act, clear of external control or influence; the personal control of Will to direct intention.

Self-honesty : the basic or original *alpha* state of *being* and *knowing*; clear and present total *Awareness* of-and-as *Self*, in its most basic and true proactive expression of itself as *Spirit* or *I-AM*—free of artificial attachments, perceptive filters and other emotionally-reactive or mentally-conditioned programming imposed on the human condition by the systematized physical world; the ability to experience existence without judgment.

spiritual timeline : a continuous stream of moment-to-moment *Mental Images* (or a record of experiences) that defines the "past" of a spiritual being (or *Alpha-Spirit*) and which includes impressions (*imprints, &tc.*) from all life-incarnations and significant spiritual events the being has encountered; in Systemology, also "*backtrack.*"

Spheres of Existence : a series of *eight* concentric circles, rings or spheres (each larger than the former) that is overlaid onto the Standard Model of Beta-Existence to demonstrate the dynamic systems of existence extending out from the POV of Self (often as a "body") at the *First Sphere*; these are given in the basic eightfold systems as: *Self*, *Home/Family*, *Groups*, *Humanity*, *Life on Earth*, *Physical Universe*, *Spiritual Universe* and *Infinity-Divinity.*

Systemology : a modern tradition of applied religious philosophy and spiritual technology based on *Arcane Tablets* (in combination with "*general systemology*" and "*games theory*") developed in the New Age underground by Joshua Free in 2011 as an advanced futurist extension of the *Mardukite Research Org.*; also known as "*Mardukite Systemology,*" "*Metahuman Systemology*" and "*Spiritual Systemology.*"

terminal (node) : a point, end, or mass, on a line; a connection point for closing an electric circuit, such as a post on a battery terminating at each end of its own systematic function; a point of connectivity with other points; in systems, a contact point of interaction; a point of interaction with other points.

turbulence : a quality or state of distortion or disturbance that creates irregularity of a flow or pattern; the quality or state of aberration on a line (such as ragged edges) or the emotional "turbulent feelings" attached to a particular flow or terminal node; a violent, haphazard or disharmonious commotion (such as in the ebb of gusts and lulls of wind action).

validation : a reinforcement of agreements or considerations as being "real."

viewpoint : see *"point-of-view" (POV)*.

willingness : the state of conscious Self-determined ability and interest (directed attention) to *Be, Do* or *Have*; a Self-determined consideration to reach, face up to (*confront*) or manage some "mass" or energy; the extent to which an individual considers themselves able to participate, act or communicate along some line, to put attention or intention on the line, or to produce (create) an effect.

ZU : the ancient Sumerian cuneiform sign for the archaic verb—*"to know," "knowingness"* or *"awareness"*; in *Mardukite Zuism and Systemology*, the active energy/matter of the "Spiritual Universe" (AN) experienced as a *Lifeforce* or *consciousness* that imbues living forms extant in the "Physical Universe" (KI); *"Spiritual Life Energy"*; energy demonstrated by the WILL of an actualized *Alpha-Spirit* in the "Spiritual Universe" (AN), which impinges its *Awareness* into the Physical Universe (KI), animating/controlling *Life* for its experience of *beta-existence* along an individual Alpha-Spirit's personal *Identity-continuum*, called a *ZU-line*.

Zu-Line : a theoretical construct in *Mardukite*

Zuism and Systemology demonstrating *Spiritual Life Energy* (*ZU*) as a personal individual "continuum" of Awareness interacting with all Spheres of Existence on the Standard Model of Systemology; a spectrum of potential variations and interactions of a monistic continuum or singular *Spiritual Life Energy* demonstrated on the Standard Model; an energetic channel of potential POV and "locations" of Beingness, demonstrated in early Systemology materials as an individual Alpha-Spirit's personal *Identity- continuum*, potentially connecting *Awareness* of *Self* with "*Infinity*" simultaneous with all points considered in existence; a symbolic demonstration of the "*Life-line*" on which *Awareness (ZU)* extends from the direction of the "Spiritual Universe" (AN) in its true original *alpha state* through an entire possible range of activity resulting in its *beta state* and control of a *genetic-entity* occupying the *Physical Universe (KI)*.

Zu-Vision : the true and basic (*Alpha*) Point-of-View (perspective, POV) maintained by *Self* as *Alpha-Spirit* outside boundaries or considerations of the *Human Condition* and *exterior* to beta-existence reality agreements with the Physical Universe; a POV of Self *as* "a unit of Spiritual Awareness" that exists independent of a "body" and entrapment in a *Human Condition*; "spirit vision" in its truest sense.

Fundamentals of Systemology
in six
Basic Course Lesson Booklets

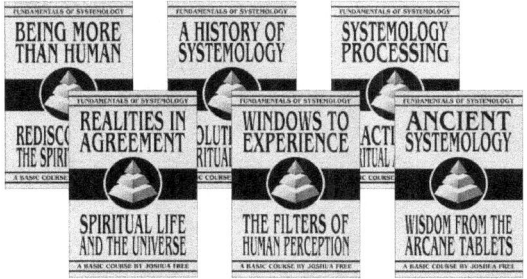

Also
available
as a
six-in-one
hardcover
edition!

THE SYSTEMOL

Seekers and students of the *Basic Course* and *Professional Course* will also be interested in the *Systemology Core Research Series*. These eight volumes are a complete chronological record of the Mardukite New Thought developments from the Systemology Society, published in 2019 through 2023.

The *Systemology Core* begins with the first professional publication released when the *Mardukite Systemology Society* emerged from the underground in 2019, with: *"The Tablets of Destiny Revelation."*

OGY PATHWAY

The Tablets of Destiny Revelation:
How Long-Lost Anunnaki Wisdom
Can Change the Fate of Humanity

Crystal Clear: *Handbook for Seekers*

Metahuman Destinations (2 *volumes*)

Imaginomicon:
Approaching Gateways to Higher Universes

Way of the Wizard: *Utilitarian Systemology*

Systemology-180: *Fast-Track to Ascension*

Systemology Backtrack:
Reclaiming Spiritual Power & Past-Life Memory

PUBLISHED BY THE **JOSHUA FREE** IMPRINT REPRESENTING

The Mardukite Academy of Systemology

THE JOSHUA FREE IMPRINT
JFI PUBLICATIONS

MARDUKITE
ZUISM

mardukite.com